Easy Mandala

a
Coloring Book for Beginners

Coloring sections purchased from adobe photostock

Coloring books are a creat tool to help you de-stress and relax and there are many beautiful and intricate mandalas to choose from.

But sometimes we don't have the time, patience or motor skills to sit down to color a mandala for several hours or days at a time.

Easy Mandala is here to help you find the joy of coloring, even if you don't have much time, patience or have some difficulties with coloring intricate designs.

Enjoy, relax, have fun.

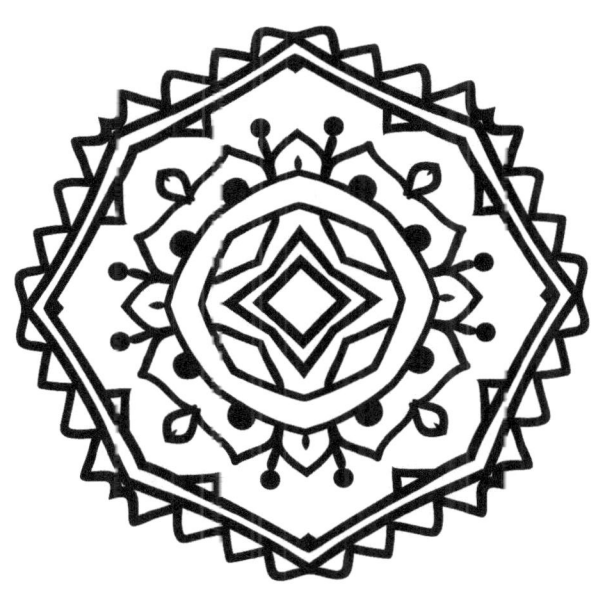

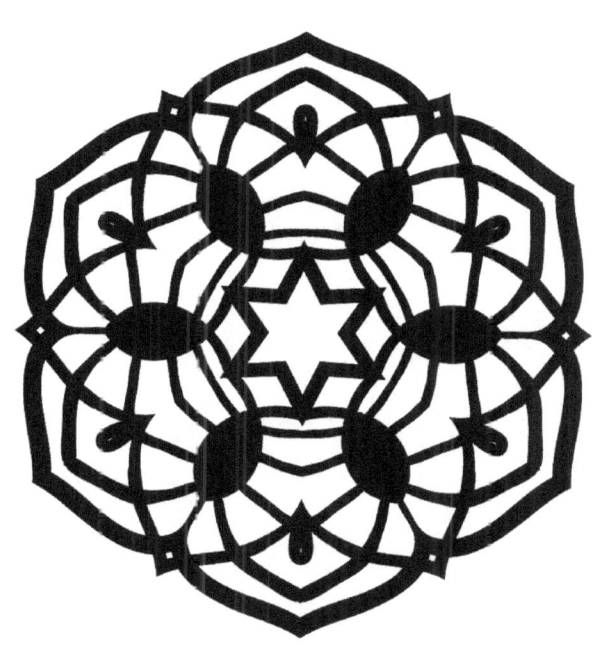

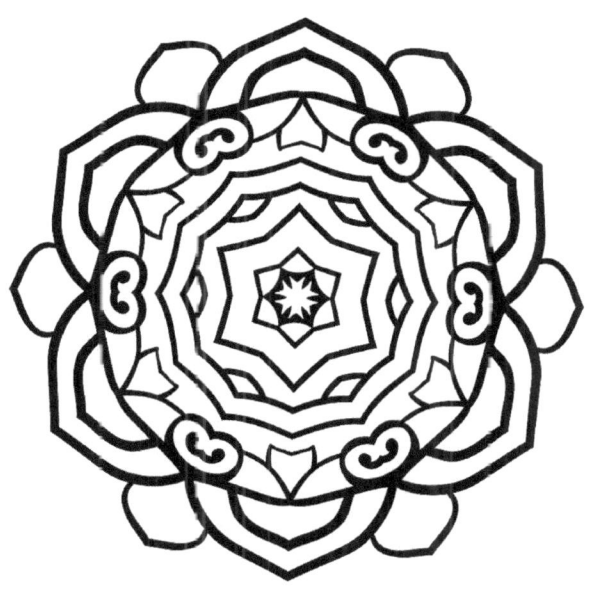

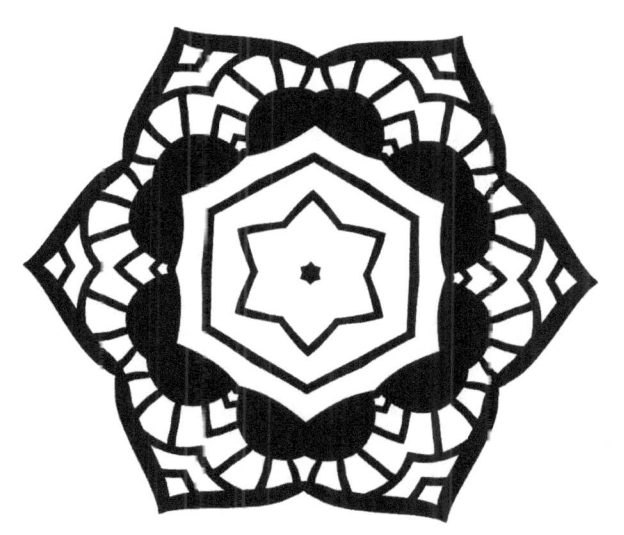

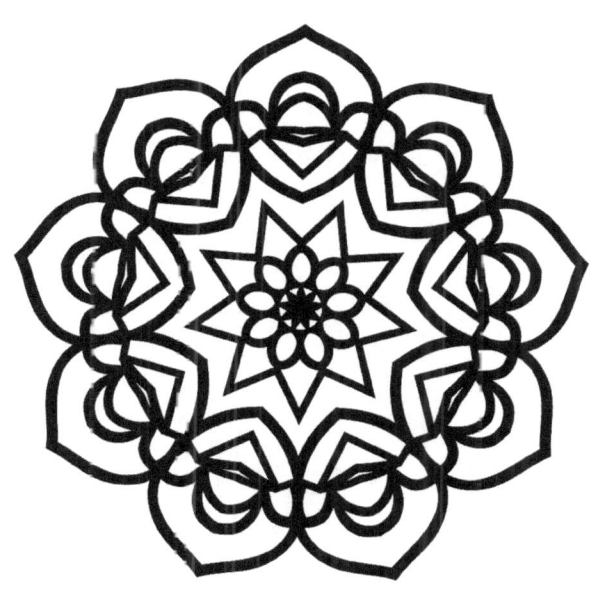

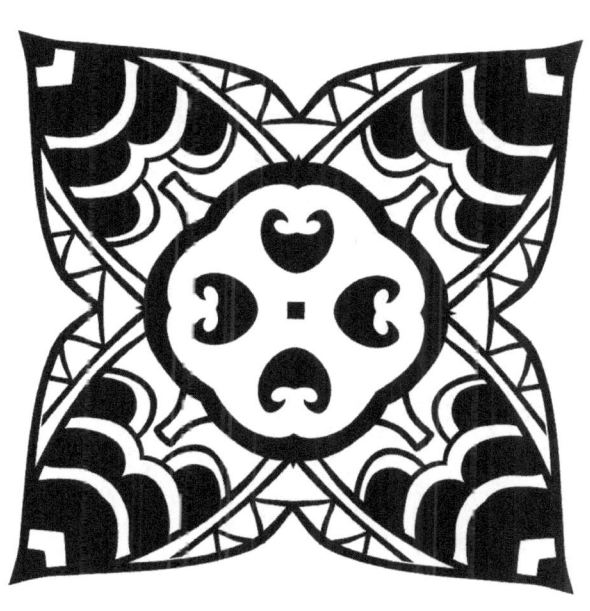

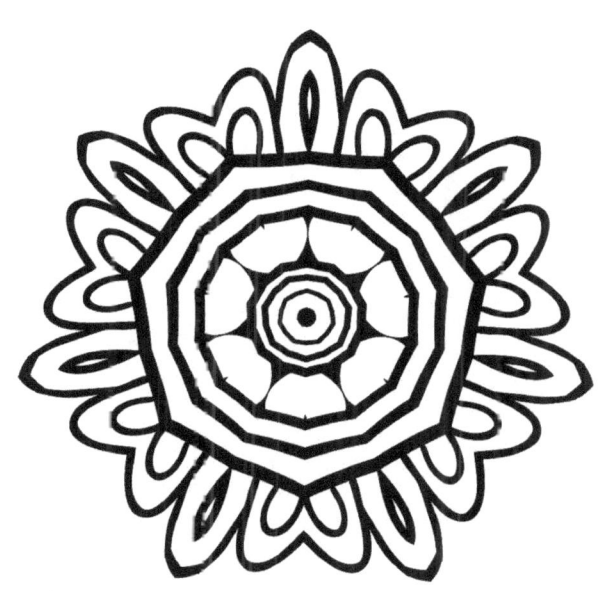

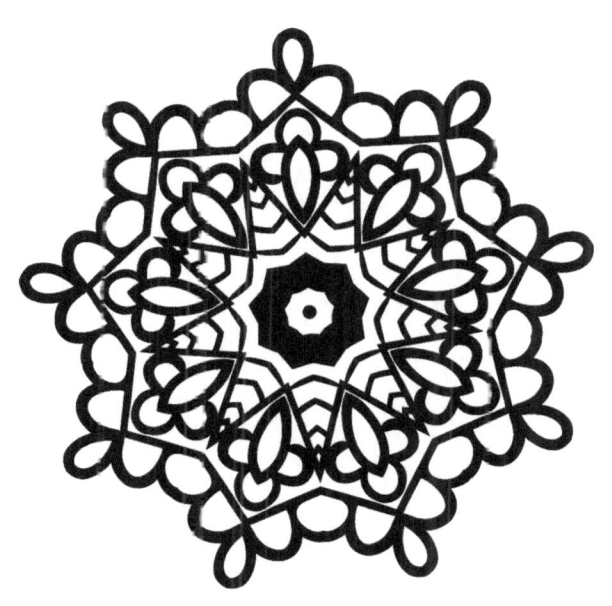

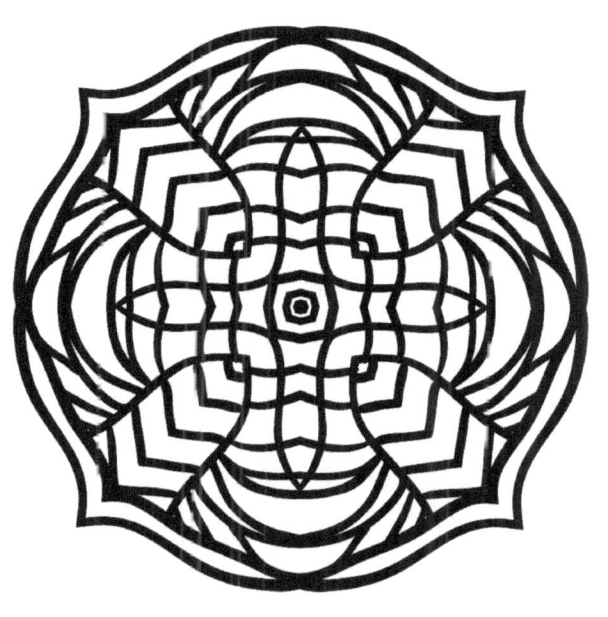

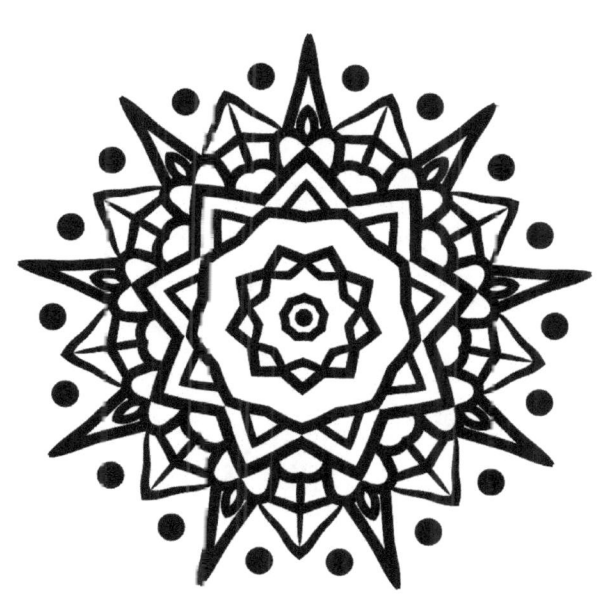

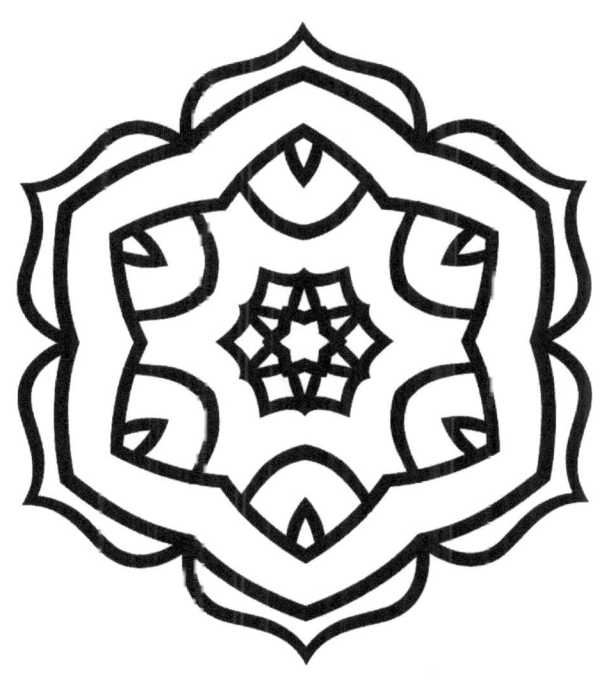

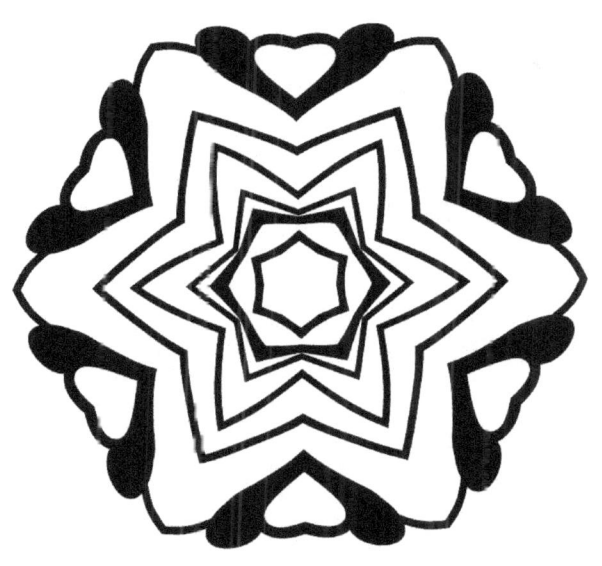

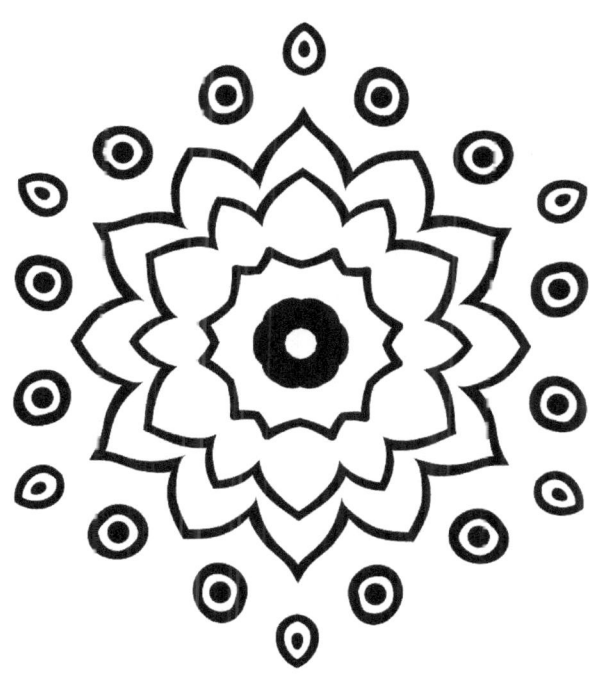

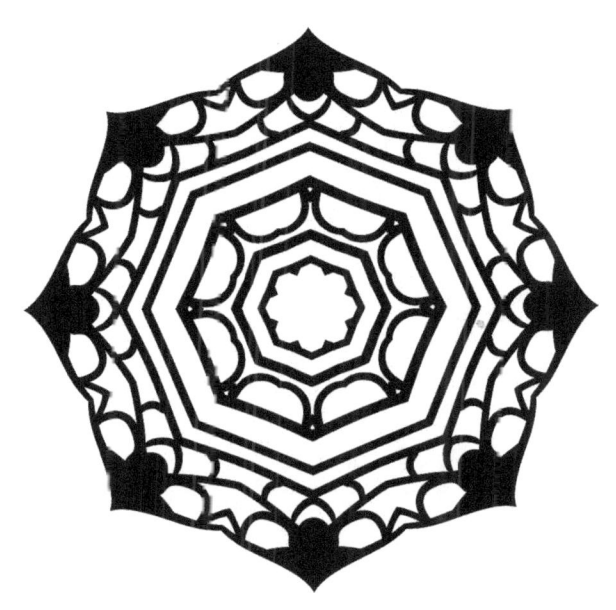

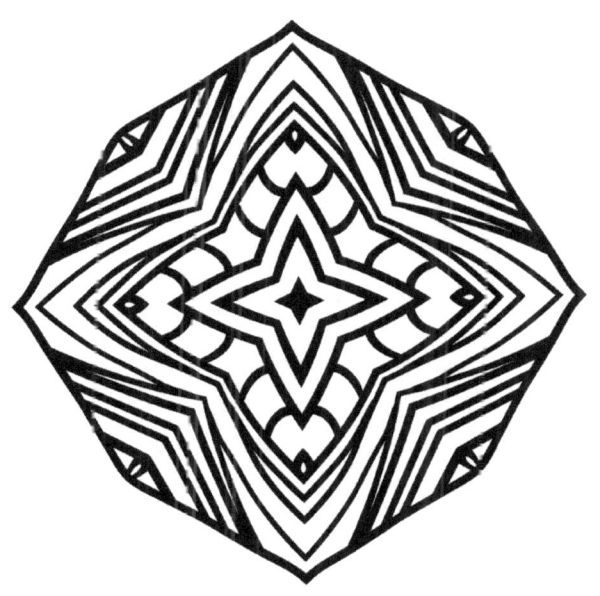

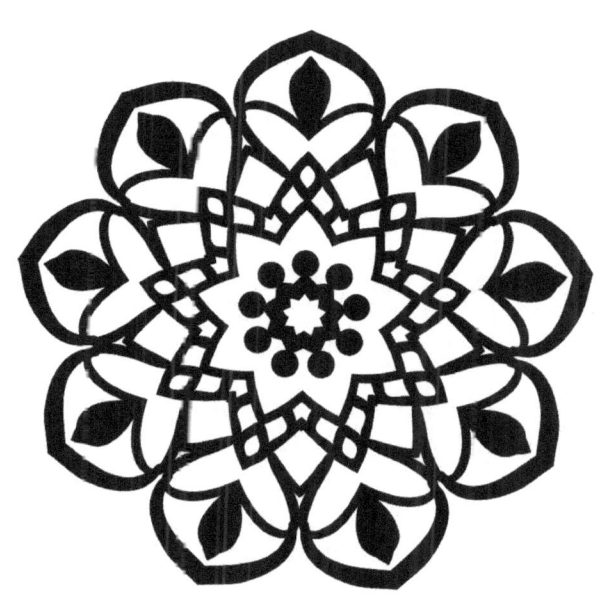

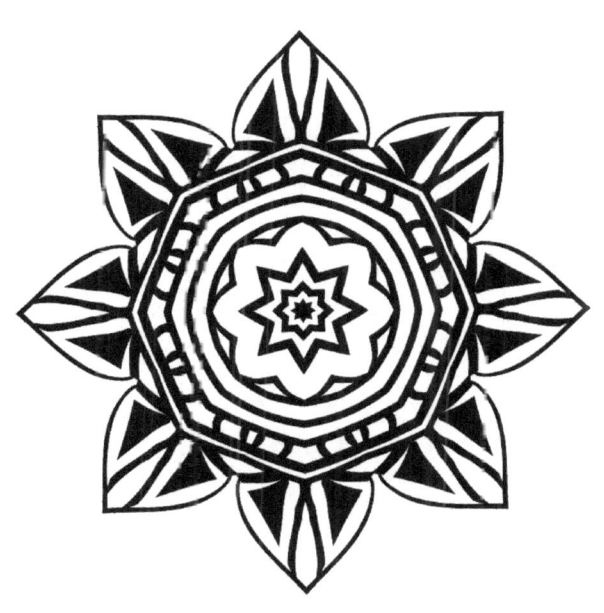

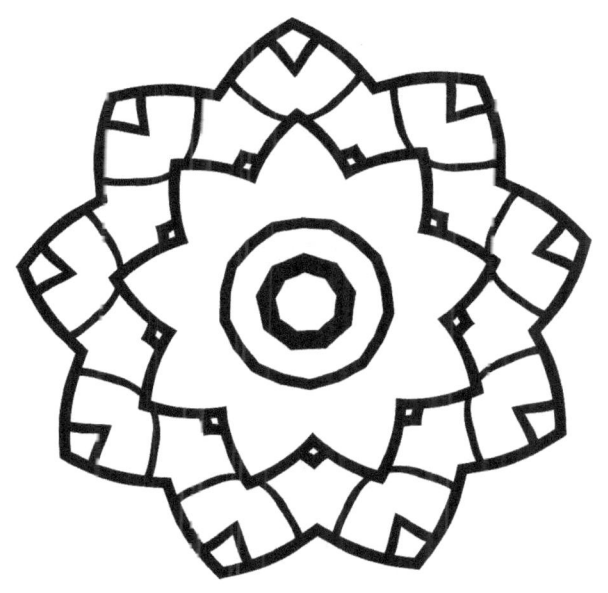